Detroit Lions

BY
JUSTIN PETERSEN

MEDIA ENHANCED BOOKS
AV2
BY WEIGL

AV² provides enriched content that supplements and complements this book. Weigl's AV² books strive to create inspired learning and engage young minds in a total learning experience.

Your AV² Media Enhanced books come alive with...

 Audio
Listen to sections of the book read aloud.

 Key Words
Study vocabulary, and complete a matching word activity.

 Video
Watch informative video clips.

 Quizzes
Test your knowledge.

 Embedded Weblinks
Gain additional information for research.

 Slide Show
View images and captions, and prepare a presentation.

 Try This!
Complete activities and hands-on experiments.

... and much, much more!

Go to **www.av2books.com**, and enter this book's unique code.

BOOK CODE

E 1 8 3 1 2 6

AV² by Weigl brings you media enhanced books that support active learning.

Published by AV² by Weigl
350 5ᵗʰ Avenue, 59ᵗʰ Floor
New York, NY 10118
Websites: www.av2books.com   www.weigl.com

Library of Congress Control Number: 2014931149

ISBN 978-1-4896-0822-2 (hardcover)
ISBN 978-1-4896-0824-6 (single user ebook)
ISBN 978-1-4896-0825-3 (multi user ebook)

Printed in the United States of America in North Mankato, Minnesota
1 2 3 4 5 6 7 8 9 0   18 17 16 15 14

042014
WEP150314

Project Coordinator Aaron Carr
Art Director Terry Paulhus

Photo Credits
Every reasonable effort has been made to trace ownership and to obtain permission to reprint copyright material. The publishers would be pleased to have any errors or omissions brought to their attention so that they may be corrected in subsequent printings.

Weigl acknowledges Getty Images as its primary image supplier for this title.

Detroit Lions

CONTENTS

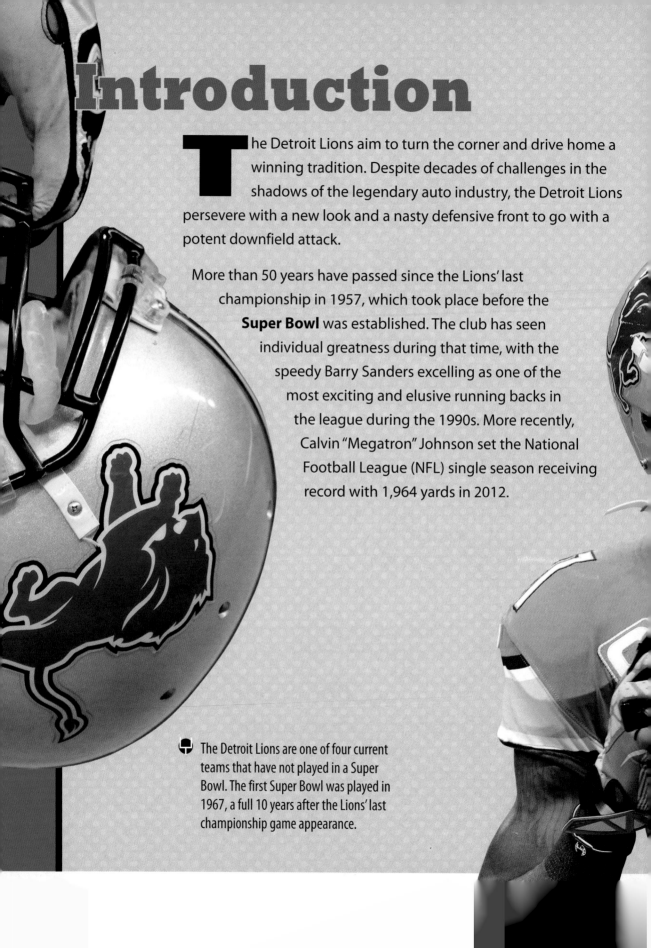

Introduction

The Detroit Lions aim to turn the corner and drive home a winning tradition. Despite decades of challenges in the shadows of the legendary auto industry, the Detroit Lions persevere with a new look and a nasty defensive front to go with a potent downfield attack.

More than 50 years have passed since the Lions' last championship in 1957, which took place before the **Super Bowl** was established. The club has seen individual greatness during that time, with the speedy Barry Sanders excelling as one of the most exciting and elusive running backs in the league during the 1990s. More recently, Calvin "Megatron" Johnson set the National Football League (NFL) single season receiving record with 1,964 yards in 2012.

The Detroit Lions are one of four current teams that have not played in a Super Bowl. The first Super Bowl was played in 1967, a full 10 years after the Lions' last championship game appearance.

The Lions have struggled to topple the league's elite, failing to reach the **playoffs** for 12 straight years after Sanders retired. Lions owner William Clay Ford, Sr. hopes his club has finally found their claws, with head coach Jim Caldwell at the helm.

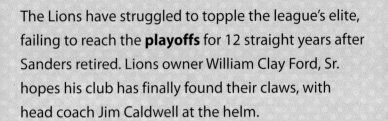

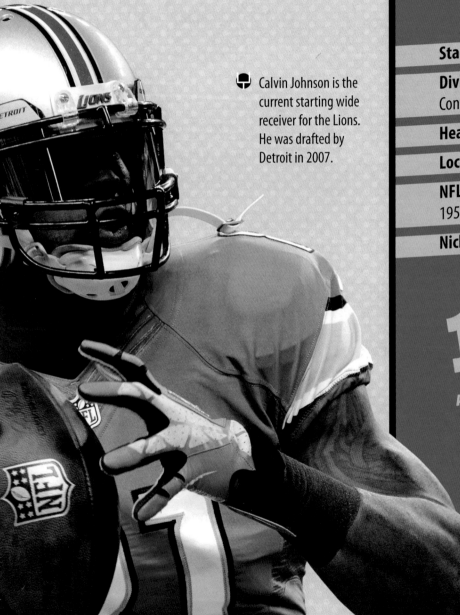

Calvin Johnson is the current starting wide receiver for the Lions. He was drafted by Detroit in 2007.

Stadium Ford Field

Division National Football Conference (NFC) North

Head coach Jim Caldwell

Location Detroit, Michigan

NFL championships 1935, 1952, 1953, 1957

Nicknames None

15
Playoff Appearances

4
NFL Championships

4
Division Championships

History

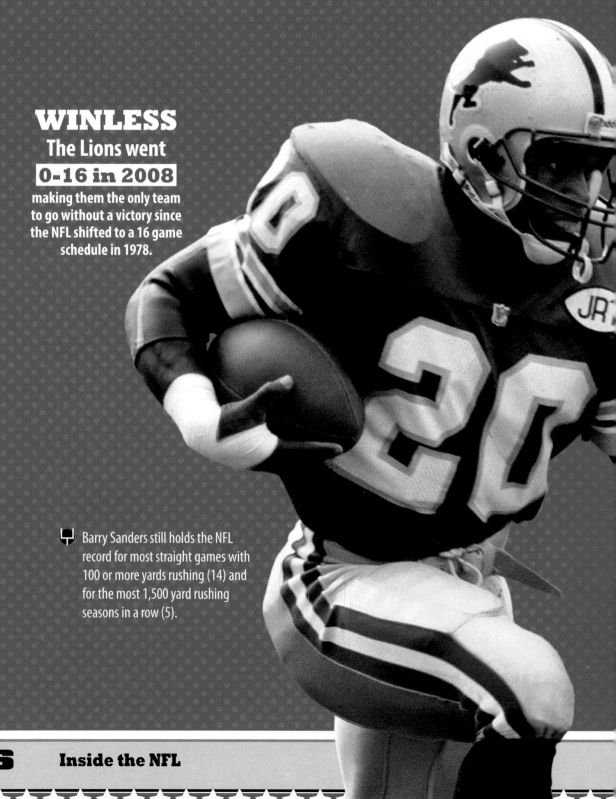

WINLESS

The Lions went **0-16 in 2008** making them the only team to go without a victory since the NFL shifted to a 16 game schedule in 1978.

Barry Sanders still holds the NFL record for most straight games with 100 or more yards rushing (14) and for the most 1,500 yard rushing seasons in a row (5).

The Detroit Lions were founded in 1929 as the Spartans in Portsmouth, Ohio. The club represented the smallest market in the league and participated in the first league playoff game. In 1934, the franchise was sold to George Richards, from Detroit, who changed the name to the Lions to honor the "monarch of the jungle." The move proved successful, and the Lions defeated the New York Giants in the 1935 league championship. More wins followed. The Lions won back-to-back titles in 1952 and 1953. They added another in 1957. Icons like tackle Lou Creekmur, inducted to the Pro Football **Hall of Fame** in 1996, established the Lions' reputation as a hard-nosed outfit. The 1960s, 1970s, and 1980s featured a number of standout performers, but did not result in any championships.

Fans remember the 1990s as Barry Sanders' era. Sanders won four straight NFL rushing titles, while his nifty moves and ability to start and stop at full speed became legendary. In 1991, Detroit reached the NFC Championship. Despite falling to the eventual champion Washington Redskins, this was Detroit's finest modern day season. After going winless in 2008, Detroit is on the right track as they reached the playoffs in 2011 for the first time in 12 years.

Lem Barney never left Detroit after his playing days, and remains active with many worthwhile causes, including mentoring inner city youth.

The Stadium

└ Ford Field seats 65,000 fans.

The Lions' current home, Ford Field, is classic and modern. Its architecture both lights up the fan experience and pays tribute to the classic automobile culture of the city. The stadium was built in 2002. Located in downtown Detroit, it rocks with 65,000 roaring fans and offers a unique experience to the spectators. Thanks to glass paneling, the stadium is able to let a good amount of light in, despite featuring a fixed roof. The six-story-tall atrium faces south, and offers a magnificent view of Detroit's skyline.

Entering the 2013 season, attendance at Ford Field had increased in each of the previous three years.

The entire south wall of the stadium is in fact one of the walls of the old Hudson's warehouse that has been restored. Hudson was a well known American automobile maker during the early 20th century. On the top of the 132 suites, the venue also offers 8,500 padded club seats that come in a package featuring upgraded food options, a private parking spot, and private lounges.

A variety of food and drinks are served, headlined by Ford Field's own Victory Knot, a two-pound pretzel!

Where They Play

CANADA

30 Washington

Oregon

Montana

North Dakota

Minnesota

Lake Superior

Idaho

23 → Wisconsin

22

South Dakota

Wyoming

Iowa

24

29

Nevada

Utah

Nebraska

13 Illinois

15

California

Colorado

14

Kansas

Missouri

UNITED STATES

31

16

Arizona

New Mexico

Oklahoma

Arkansas

32

Texas

17

Pacific Ocean

12

Louisiana

Mississippi

27

Alaska

0   500 Miles
0   500 km

Hawai'i

MEXICO

0 100 Miles
0 100 km

Gulf of Mexico

AMERICAN FOOTBALL CONFERENCE

EAST	NORTH	SOUTH	WEST
1 Gillette Stadium	5 FirstEnergy Stadium	9 EverBank Field	13 Arrowhead Stadium
2 MetLife Stadium	6 Heinz Field	10 LP Field	14 Sports Authority Field at Mile High
3 Ralph Wilson Stadium	7 M&T Bank Stadium	11 Lucas Oil Stadium	15 O.co Coliseum
4 Sun Life Stadium	8 Paul Brown Stadium	12 NRG Stadium	16 Qualcomm Stadium

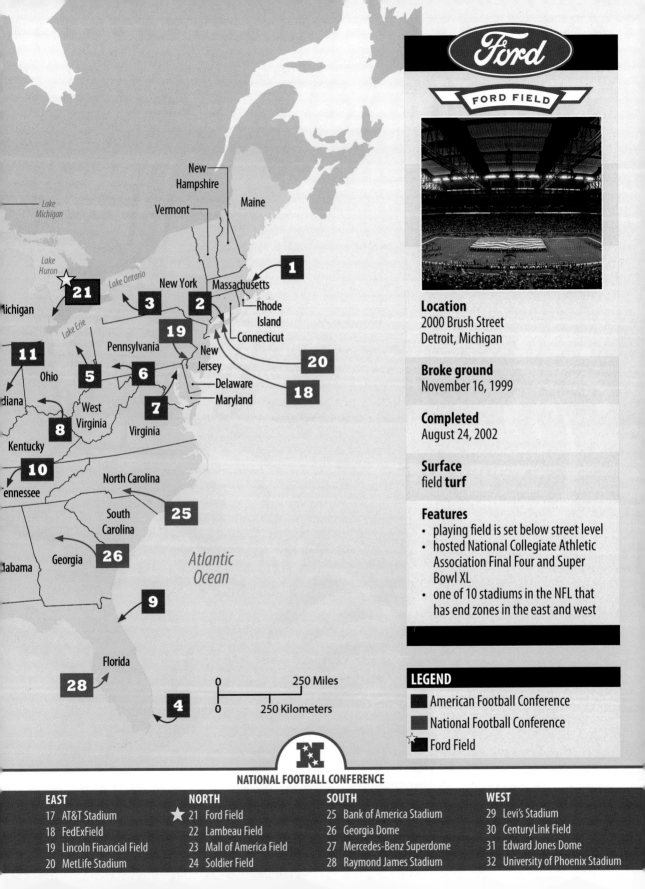

FORD FIELD

Location
2000 Brush Street
Detroit, Michigan

Broke ground
November 16, 1999

Completed
August 24, 2002

Surface
field **turf**

Features
- playing field is set below street level
- hosted National Collegiate Athletic Association Final Four and Super Bowl XL
- one of 10 stadiums in the NFL that has end zones in the east and west

LEGEND
- American Football Conference
- National Football Conference
- ☆ Ford Field

Lake Michigan
Lake Huron
Lake Ontario
Lake Erie

New Hampshire
Vermont
Maine
New York
Massachusetts
Rhode Island
Connecticut
Michigan
Pennsylvania
New Jersey
Delaware
Maryland
Ohio
Indiana
West Virginia
Virginia
Kentucky
Tennessee
North Carolina
South Carolina
Georgia
Alabama
Florida

Atlantic Ocean

250 Miles
250 Kilometers

NATIONAL FOOTBALL CONFERENCE

EAST
17 AT&T Stadium
18 FedExField
19 Lincoln Financial Field
20 MetLife Stadium

NORTH
☆ 21 Ford Field
22 Lambeau Field
23 Mall of America Field
24 Soldier Field

SOUTH
25 Bank of America Stadium
26 Georgia Dome
27 Mercedes-Benz Superdome
28 Raymond James Stadium

WEST
29 Levi's Stadium
30 CenturyLink Field
31 Edward Jones Dome
32 University of Phoenix Stadium

The Uniforms

The Lions wear **HONOLULU BLUE** uniforms, which is named for the color of the waves in Hawai'i.

Matthew Stafford was one of four rookies who started Detroit's 2009 opener.

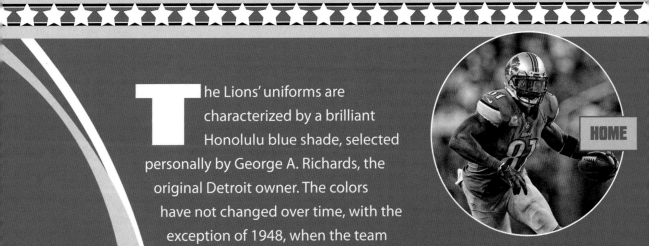

The Lions' uniforms are characterized by a brilliant Honolulu blue shade, selected personally by George A. Richards, the original Detroit owner. The colors have not changed over time, with the exception of 1948, when the team played in a maroon jersey. Coach Bo McMillin, a former Indiana University coach, made that decision. The team restored its traditional scheme the following year.

In 2003, the team added a black trim to the uniforms to give a better outline to the whole design. The away uniforms are white with blue lines on the arms. The Lions have also had a black **alternate jersey** between 2003 and 2008.

NFL uniforms are designed to be lightweight and breathable, so players can make great plays, and celebrate, with ease.

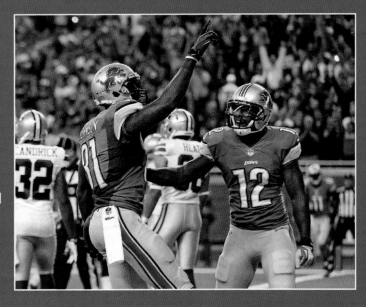

The Helmets

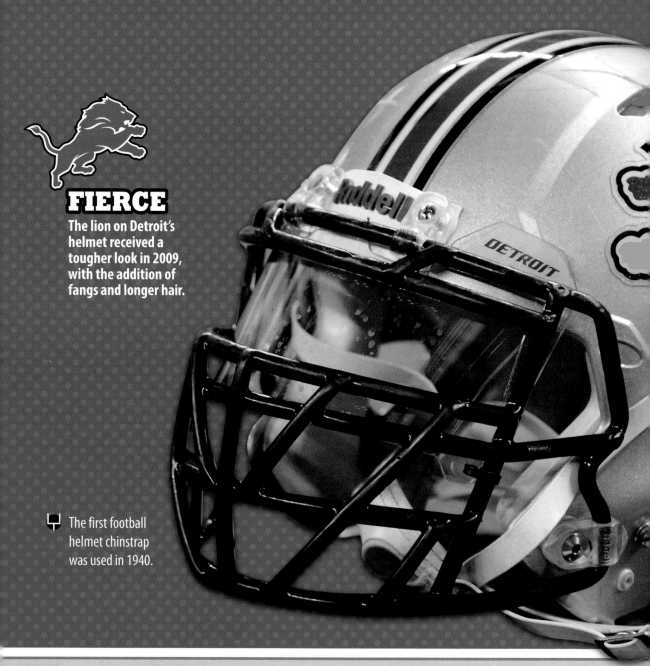

FIERCE

The lion on Detroit's helmet received a tougher look in 2009, with the addition of fangs and longer hair.

The first football helmet chinstrap was used in 1940.

Lions helmets feature a blue lion reared up on its haunches and ready to attack. Until recently, only the shape of the lion itself was visible, but the design now includes more details, including the lion's eye and claws. This **logo** scheme has changed four times since the franchise moved to Detroit. The original logo featured football player on a golden lion's back.

The practice of including logos on helmets, in fact, did not appear in the NFL until the end of the 1940s, and it was not until 1961 that the Lions franchise itself finally included their symbol on the helmet's design. Before that, the Lions' design changed considerably in terms of color, from brown to blue to red and even to gold. Lions helmets have been gray since 1953. The team introduced blue stripes in 1961.

The NFL did not require players to wear helmets until 1943.

The Coaches

14 During Jim Caldwell's first season as head coach for the Indianapolis Colts in 2009, his team raced out to a fantastic 14-0 start.

Before Caldwell became the Lions' head coach, he was the quarterbacks coach for the 2013 Super Bowl champion, Baltimore Ravens.

Lions coaches have struggled to repeat the recipe that last earned the club a title in 1957. While their efforts have not resulted in wins, each new face has delivered an entertaining persona and memorable battle cry. Fans watched Wayne Fontes orchestrate a great rushing offense. Bobby Ross stressed hard-nosed defense. Steve Mariucci tested the West Coast Offense in middle America.

WAYNE FONTES

Fontes was hired by the Lions during the middle of the 1988 season following the departure of Darryl Rogers. Under his guidance, the Lions made the playoffs four times, reaching the NFC Championship in 1991. Fontes was voted NFL's Coach of the Year in 1992.

BOBBY ROSS

Bobby Ross took the helm of the Lions in 1997. He wanted to instill a more physical way to play and brought more discipline to a team that had yet to live up to its potential. Ross was desperate to change things but he ultimately did not manage to revolutionize the culture of a team that was "playing only for paychecks."

JIM CALDWELL

Following the 2013 season, the Lions hired Jim Caldwell, a proven **passing game** coach, to guide the squad. Caldwell built a stellar reputation under Tony Dungy with the Indianapolis Colts as Peyton Manning's quarterback coach. Caldwell eventually inherited the head coaching post and guided the Colts to a Super Bowl appearance.

The Mascot

Roary the Lion claims his paws are bigger than basketball great Shaquille O'Neal and his size 22 shoes.

Roary is Detroit's favorite lion. Ten paws tall, full of hair and shiny teeth, Roary certainly is an adorable feline. He is very secretive about his love life. No one knows if he shares his den with a lioness. His best pal is the other local furry legend, the Detroit Tigers' mascot, Paws.

Roary trains a lot to be in a good shape and follows the NFL Fuel Up to Play 60 program, and recommends it to anybody with professional football dreams. Roary is also the "spokeslion" of the Detroit Lions Kids Club and is involved in local educational programs.

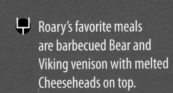

🏈 Roary has been leading fans in cheering on the Lions for many years, but he will not say how old he is.

🏈 Roary's favorite meals are barbecued Bear and Viking venison with melted Cheeseheads on top.

Legends of the Past

Many great players have suited up in the Lions' blue and silver. A few of them have become icons of the team and the city it represents.

Dick LeBeau

Position Cornerback
Seasons 14 (1959–1972)
Born September 9, 1937, in London, Ohio

Dick LeBeau is widely considered the greatest defensive back in Lions' history. Despite a rough start, the cornerback was cut by the Cleveland Browns before the Lions picked him up, LeBeau earned a starting position by the end of his rookie year in Detroit. Teaming with Dick "Night Train" Lane, Yale Lary, and Lem Barney, the Lions' defensive backfield terrorized opposing quarterbacks during the 1960s. LeBeau snatched 62 interceptions for 762 return yards and three touchdowns during his 14-year career. LeBeau played in 171 straight games, the most by a cornerback in NFL history. LeBeau was inducted into the Pro Football Hall of Fame in 2010.

Joe Schmidt

Joe Schmidt spent his entire professional career with the Lions. Drafted in the 7th round, Schmidt helped Detroit claim their second league title in a row, and went on to become a team captain in 1956. His style was "clean but mean" and he showed great intelligence while playing the game. The fierce linebacker was voted the best defensive player in the league in 1957. He played in 10 **Pro Bowls**, and made the **All-Pro** first team eight times. He played through injury for a good part of his career, making him one of the toughest players to play the game. He wore the number 56, a number that has since been retired in Detroit.

Position Linebacker
Seasons 13 (1953–1965)
Born January 19, 1952, in Pittsburgh, Pennsylvania

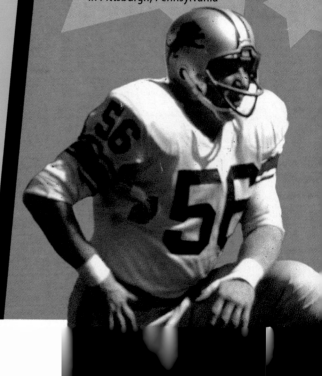

Chris Spielman

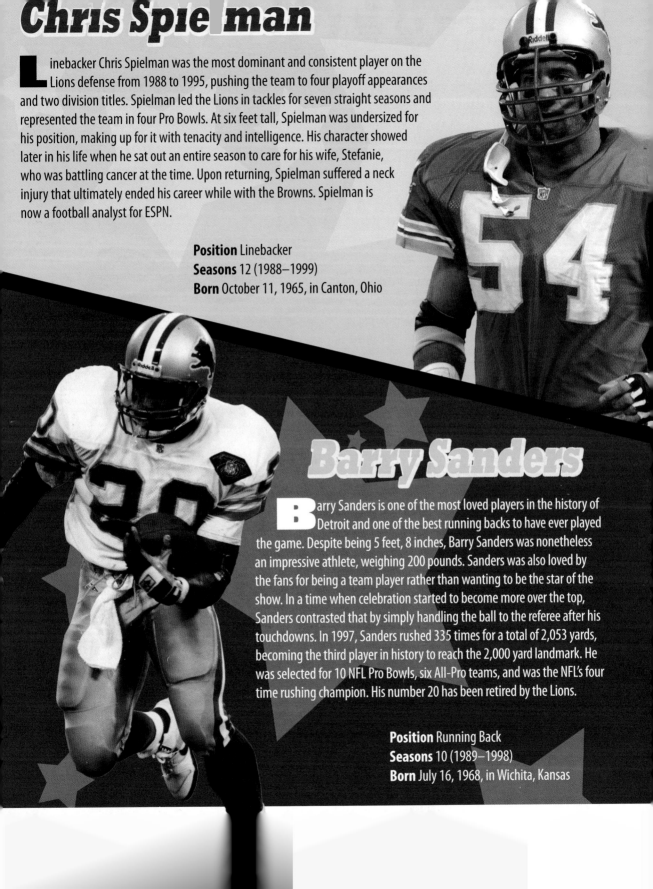

Linebacker Chris Spielman was the most dominant and consistent player on the Lions defense from 1988 to 1995, pushing the team to four playoff appearances and two division titles. Spielman led the Lions in tackles for seven straight seasons and represented the team in four Pro Bowls. At six feet tall, Spielman was undersized for his position, making up for it with tenacity and intelligence. His character showed later in his life when he sat out an entire season to care for his wife, Stefanie, who was battling cancer at the time. Upon returning, Spielman suffered a neck injury that ultimately ended his career while with the Browns. Spielman is now a football analyst for ESPN.

Position Linebacker
Seasons 12 (1988–1999)
Born October 11, 1965, in Canton, Ohio

Barry Sanders

Barry Sanders is one of the most loved players in the history of Detroit and one of the best running backs to have ever played the game. Despite being 5 feet, 8 inches, Barry Sanders was nonetheless an impressive athlete, weighing 200 pounds. Sanders was also loved by the fans for being a team player rather than wanting to be the star of the show. In a time when celebration started to become more over the top, Sanders contrasted that by simply handling the ball to the referee after his touchdowns. In 1997, Sanders rushed 335 times for a total of 2,053 yards, becoming the third player in history to reach the 2,000 yard landmark. He was selected for 10 NFL Pro Bowls, six All-Pro teams, and was the NFL's four time rushing champion. His number 20 has been retired by the Lions.

Position Running Back
Seasons 10 (1989–1998)
Born July 16, 1968, in Wichita, Kansas

Stars of Today

Today's Lions team is made up of many young, talented players who have proven that they are among the best players in the league.

Matthew Stafford

Matthew Stafford is one of the most gifted quarterbacks of his generation. He signed a contract for the Lions in 2009 that made him one of the biggest earners in the NFL without having played a single professional game. Stafford has earned the attention by helping Detroit build one of the most potent passing attacks in the NFL. Stafford has reached 15,000 yards passing faster than any other quarterback in NFL history, surpassing that mark in just 53 games.

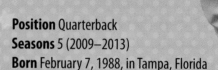

Position Quarterback
Seasons 5 (2009–2013)
Born February 7, 1988, in Tampa, Florida

Calvin Johnson

Calvin Johnson is nicknamed Megatron for his imposing stature (6 feet, 5 inches and 236.3 pounds). Despite seeing constant double coverage, Johnson is impossible to stop. He set the NFL record for receiving yards in 2012, with 1,964, a record previously held by Jerry Rice. Johnson ran a 4.35 40-yard sprint at the NFL Scouting Combine and he has a cat-like agility, making him one of the best wide receivers in the league. Experts predicted that Johnson would be one of the best receivers to play the game. In his career, he has accomplished just that.

Position Wide Receiver
Seasons 7 (2007–2013)
Born September 29, 1985, in Newman, Georgia

Reggie Bush

Reggie Bush is one of the most electric players in the NFL. He has the ability to change the game with a single reception or carry. He is also one of the most versatile players in the league, with top skills as a rusher, pass catcher and return man. Bush won Super Bowl XLIV with New Orleans. He then signed with the Dolphins in 2011, adapting his game to become a more traditional running back.

Position Running Back
Seasons 8 (2006–2013)
Born March 2, 1985, in Spring Valley, California

Ezekiel Ansah

Ghanaian born Ezekiel "Ziggy" Ansah became acquainted with the NFL quite late in his life. He played soccer in his early childhood and was also very keen on basketball. Ansah was accepted at Brigham Young University (BYU) in 2008, thanks to his academic record. At BYU, Ansah played football for the first time and, surprisingly, made the team. He went on to play with the Cougars from 2010 to 2012. Ansah's career probably would not have started if not for his outstanding performance at the 2013 Senior Bowl, where he dominated. He was drafted fifth in the first round of the 2013 NFL Draft.

Position Defensive End
Seasons 1 (2013)
Born May 29, 1989, in Accra, Ghana

All-Time Records

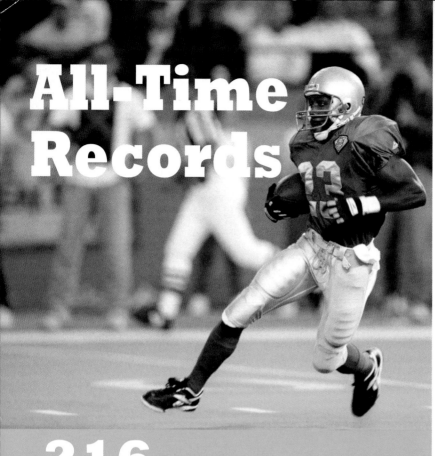

216 Career Kickoff Returns

Mel Gray holds the franchise's all-time record for most career kickoff return yards. His 216 runbacks for 5,478 yards placed him as the fifth highest return specialist of all time.

1,964 Single-season Receiving Yards

Calvin Johnson broke Jerry Rice's single-season receiving yard NFL record of 1,848 yards on December 22, 2012 against the Atlanta Falcons. Johnson finished the season with 1,964 receiving yards.

327
Most Games

Placekicker Jason Hanson spent his career with the Lions. The more than 300 games Hanson played in a Lions uniform is the NFL record for most games played with one team.

1,500
Single-season Rushing Yards

From 1994 to 1997, Barry Sanders set an NFL record for most straight seasons with 1,500 or more rushing yards. Sanders missed the mark for a fifth season by nine yards in 1998, finishing with 1,491 yards.

1,138 Career Tackles

Linebacker Chris Spielman leads the Lions in career tackles. He also holds the team's highest single-season record for 195 tackles in 1994.

Timeline

Throughout the team's history, the Detroit Lions have had many memorable events that have become defining moments for the team and its fans.

1934
The Great Depression and low revenues endangers the survival of the Spartans. George Richards, owner of the Detroit radio station WJR, buys the team, moves them to Detroit, and renames them the Detroit Lions. The name signifies that they will dominate like the king of the jungle, the lion.

1952
Quarterback Bobby Layne leads the Lions to their first championship victory in 17 years. Detroit defeats the Cleveland Browns 17-7.

1974
The Lions play their last game at Tiger Stadium, where they are defeated by the Denver Broncos 31-27. After the game, the team moves indoors to the Silverdome.

| 1930 | 1940 | 1950 | 1960 | 1970 | 1980 |

1929
This year marks the official start of the Lions as the Portsmouth, Ohio Spartans. The Spartans receive league membership in 1930 by the NFL after the residents of Portsmouth funded construction of the team's field, which was named Universal Stadium.

1957
During the Western Conference championship game against the San Francisco 49ers, Tobin Rote steps in for an injured Bobby Layne at halftime. Rote rallies the Lions from a 20 point deficit to a 31-27 win. With the victory, the Lions record the team's fourth league title.

In 1961, the Lions play in the first ever Playoff Bowl against the Browns, defeating them in a close game, 17-16.

The Future
With players like Ndamukong Suh, Stafford, Johnson, Bush, Nick Fairley, Stephen Tulloch, and Brandon Pettigrew, the team has a bright future. Their pass-orientated offense should help guide them to a long awaited playoff victory, and possibly much more.

1991
The Lions suffer a 45-0 loss to the Redskins in the season's opener. Later in the year, Washington whacks them again, 41-10, in the NFC Championship game.

In 2008, the Detroit Lions become the only team to have a zero victory season since the league switched to a 16 game schedule in 1978.

1990	1995	2000	2005	2010	2015

Barry Sanders retires in 1998, ending his highlight reel career.

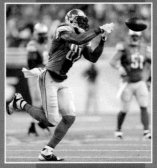

2013
Calvin Johnson sets a new Lions record for career touchdown catches with 63. Johnson is named to the 2014 Pro Bowl, but is unable to attend due to injury.

1989
Barry Sanders is drafted by the team and narrowly misses the NFL rushing title by 10 yards. This is due to his decision to sit out part of the final game because the Lions already had victory in hand.

Write a Biography

Life Story

A person's life story can be the subject of a book. This kind of book is called a biography. Biographies often describe the lives of people who have achieved great success. These people may be alive today, or they may have lived many years ago. Reading a biography can help you learn more about a great person.

Get the Facts

Use this book, and research in the library and on the Internet, to find out more about your favorite Lion. Learn as much about this player as you can. What position does he play? What are his statistics in important categories? Has he set any records? Also, be sure to write down key events in the person's life. What was his childhood like? What has he accomplished off the field? Is there anything else that makes this person special or unusual?

Use the Concept Web

A concept web is a useful research tool. Read the questions in the concept web on the following page. Answer the questions in your notebook. Your answers will help you write a biography.

Concept Web

Your Opinion
- What did you learn from the books you read in your research?
- Would you suggest these books to others?
- Was anything missing from these books?

Adulthood
- Where does this individual currently reside?
- Does he or she have a family?

Childhood
- Where and when was this person born?
- Describe his or her parents, siblings, and friends.
- Did this person grow up in unusual circumstances?

Accomplishments off the Field
- What is this person's life's work?
- Has he or she received awards or recognition for accomplishments?
- How have this person's accomplishments served others?

Write a Biography

Help and Obstacles
- Did this individual have a positive attitude?
- Did he or she receive help from others?
- Did this person have a mentor?
- Did this person face any hardships?
- If so, how were the hardships overcome?

Accomplishments on the Field
- What records does this person hold?
- What key games and plays have defined his or her career?
- What are his or her stats in categories important to his or her position?

Work and Preparation
- What was this person's education?
- What was his or her work experience?
- How does this person work; what is the process he or she uses?

Trivia Time

Take this quiz to test your knowledge of the Detroit Lions.
The answers are printed upside-down under each question.

1 When did the franchise move to Detroit?

A. 1934

2 How many NFL titles have the Lions won?

A. four

3 What is the name of the Lions' mascot?

A. Roary the Lion

4 What was the color of the team's uniform in 1948?

A. Maroon

5 What was the Lions' original team name?

A. The Spartans

6 What is the name of the Lions' current stadium, and when was it built?

A. Ford Field, the building was completed in 2002

7 Who played 327 games with the Lions?

A. Jason Hanson

8 What number was worn by legend Barry Sanders?

A. 20

9 What shade of blue are the Lions' uniforms?

A. Honolulu blue

10 What year did the Lions first have a logo on their helmets?

A. 1961

Key Words

All-Pro: an NFL player judged to be the best in his position for a given season

alternate jersey: a jersey that sports teams may wear in games instead of their home or away uniforms

hall of fame: a group of persons judged to be outstanding, as in a sport or profession

logo: a symbol that stands for a team or organization

passing game: a play in which one of the players throws the ball to a teammate

playoffs: the games played following the end of the regular season; six teams qualify: the winners of the four conferences, and the two best teams that did not finish first in their conference, called wild cards

Pro Bowl: the annual all-star game for NFL players pitting the best players in the National Football Conference against the best players in the American Football Conference

Super Bowl: the NFL's annual championship game between the winning team from the NFC and the winning team from the AFC

turf: grass and the surface layer of earth held together by its roots

Index

Log on to www.av2books.com

AV² by Weigl brings you media enhanced books that support active learning. Go to www.av2books.com, and enter the special code found on page 2 of this book. You will gain access to enriched and enhanced content that supplements and complements this book. Content includes video, audio, weblinks, quizzes, a slide show, and activities.

AV² Online Navigation

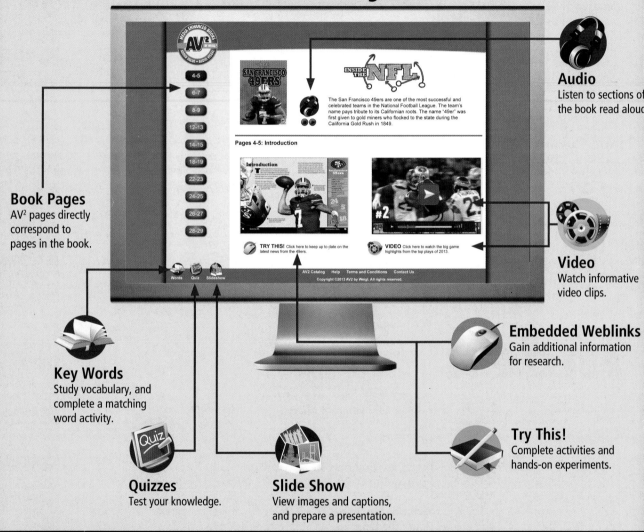

Audio
Listen to sections of the book read aloud

Book Pages
AV² pages directly correspond to pages in the book.

Video
Watch informative video clips.

Embedded Weblinks
Gain additional information for research.

Key Words
Study vocabulary, and complete a matching word activity.

Try This!
Complete activities and hands-on experiments.

Quizzes
Test your knowledge.

Slide Show
View images and captions, and prepare a presentation.

AV² was built to bridge the gap between print and digital. We encourage you to tell us what you like and what you want to see in the future.

Sign up to be an AV² Ambassador at www.av2books.com/ambassador.